D1404739

Can
you
find

Bernard Most

HARCOURT BRACE & COMPANY
San Diego   New York   London
Printed in Singapore

To my **favorite editor**
Diane D'Andrade

For giving me the **itch** to publish an idea that was **sitting** in my files for years and years, **permit** me to acknowledge Ms. Susie Mantell's November 1988 Pre-First Grade Class at Westorchard Elementary in Chappaqua, New York; and Mrs. J. Tryggestad's May 1992 Class 3Y at Woodside Elementary in Peekskill, New York; as well as countless other students and teachers for their wonderful projects based on my word-play books.

Requests for permission to make copies of any part of the work should be mailed to: Permissions Department, Harcourt Brace & Company, 8th Floor, Orlando, Florida 32887.

Library of Congress Cataloging-in-Publication Data
Most, Bernard.
Can you find it?/by Bernard Most. — 1st ed.
p. cm.
Summary: Fifteen word-play puzzles that encourage readers to find the word ''it'' in other words such as ''pitcher'' and ''mitt.''
ISBN 0-15-292872-3
1. Word games — Juvenile literature. 2. Puzzles — Juvenile literature.
[1. Word games. 2. Puzzles.] I. Title.
GV1507.W8M64   1993
793.73 — dc20   92-33691

The illustrations in this book were done in Pantone Markers on Bainbridge board 172.
The display type and text type were set in Syntax by Thompson Type, San Diego, California.
Color separations were made by Bright Arts, Ltd., Singapore.
Printed and bound by Tien Wah Press, Singapore
Production supervision by Warren Wallerstein and David Hough
Designed by Lori J. McThomas

First edition

ABCDE

You can look for **it** when you play baseball.

You'll find **it**

in your **m<u>itt</u>**!

If you look for **it**

when you're drinking juice . . .

you'll find **it**
in the **p<u>it</u>cher**!

You can look for **it**

while you're standing . . .

but you won't find **it**
till you **s<u>it</u>**!

You won't find **it**

in an empty room.

You'll find **it**
in a room that has **fur<u>it</u>ure**!

If you look for **it**

in a pet shop . . .

you'll find **it**

when you pet a **rabb<u>it</u>**!

You can look for **it**

at the ice cream store.

You'll find **it**
if you share a banana **spl<u>it</u>**!

You can look for **it**

if you like music.

You'll find **it**
in a **gu<u>i</u>tar**!

You can look for **it** in a museum.

You'll find **it** in p**s<u>it</u>tacosaurus**!

If you look for **it**

in the dark . . .

you'll find **it**

when you **switch** on the light!

You can look for **it**
in school.

You'll find **it** in **ar<u>it</u>hmetic**!

You can look for **it**

if you're an astronaut.

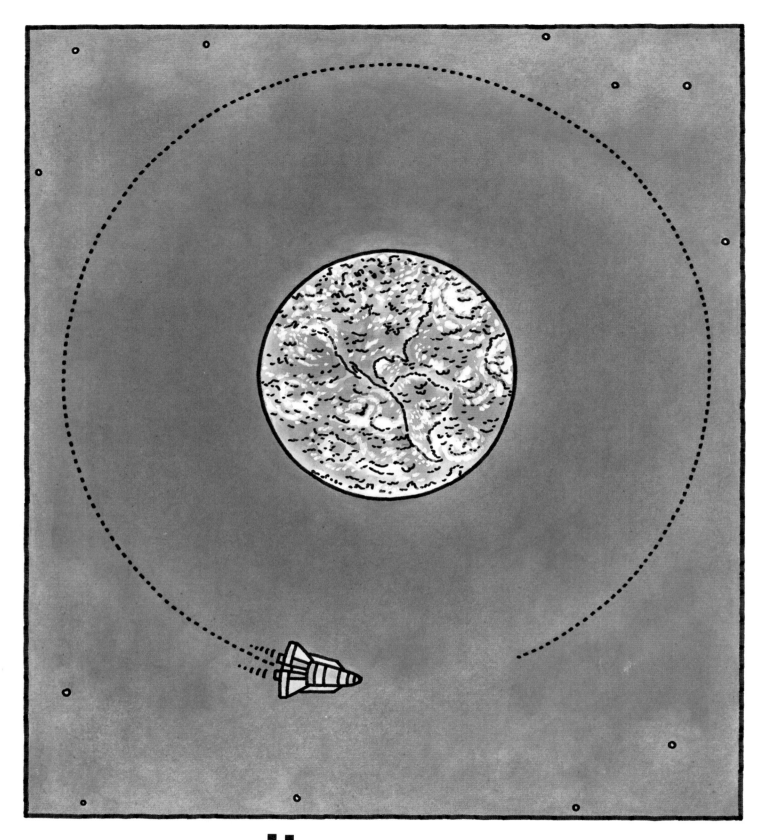

You'll find **it** when you're in **orb<u>it</u>**!

You can look for **it**
when you try on new clothes.

You'll find **it**

when something **fits**!

You can look for **it**

in the country...

but you won't find **it**

till you're in the **ci<u>t</u>y**!

You can look for **it**
when the bank is robbed.

You'll find **it**

when they catch the **band<u>it</u>**!

You can look for **it**
just before you go to sleep.

You'll find **it** on a **moonlit** night!